TITLE PAGE:

Barack Obama, Do Cyborgs Dream Of

Robotic Sheep? An American Poem

By

Mark David King

Copyright 2009 Mark David King ISBN 978-0-578-00225-5

Barack Obama, Do Cyborgs Dream Of Robotic Sheep? An American Poem

By

Mark David King

Purchase all of my books on Amazon.Com, Internet Bookstores, and Lulu.Com—

1.) How to practice White Magic

2.) Sean Hannity's theocracy; plus, Virgin Mary LIVES!

3.) About Britney Spears and male genitalia--an anthropological treatise

4.) Werewolf Slut

5.) The Season of Tara

6.) Dana Dickson battles Lindsay Lohan: Jelly Roll's Poem

Hey, I'm not a cop; I'm a player.

- Arnold Schwarzenegger -

Part One—

ONE:

Barack Obama wants to architect a plan

That will forge an awesome and unearthly man;

Moreover, not only will his own person be blessed,

Yet he will make the American soul feel caressed;

Alas, like Kennedy he is young and bright by way of charisma,

Being a stick in the eye to all racists with his enigma

That is we as Americans have evolved beyond

The lies of bigotry that at one time conned

Our Nation into not being equal,

But now we flush that down the toilet cause it's fecal,

Mattering not as much anymore,

For the black man is at America's core,

And how proud when Michael Jordan played for the dream team,

Outshining our competitors with his African-American mien,

And Larry Bird at his side—

These two merging into a blessed mulatto hide,

As it is with Barack Obama,

Him being such a gentleman that he'd love your mama;

Indeed, today Martin Luther King Jr. does have more than a dream,

For the union of black and white is now frothing over like nectar cream,

And we should all raise our glasses high,

Toasting the pride of God since racism is beginning to die

As we morph into more understanding creatures,

Not minding if other folk have different features;

Indeed, America's eyes now do look further and deeper,

Having developed a vision that is sublime and clearer,

Outgrowing a tear on a child that is a specter of the past,

Them having witnessed their black father in a noose breathe his last

Breath, as it was thieved away

By the spirit of hate that did dismay;

However, as if infused by the love of God,

Now to the black man we do give a nod,

Trusting in Barack Obama to run our great country

That went through times tough and krunky,

Yet not even Bill Clinton will have such a presidency,

For Mr. Obama has not such an adulterous tendency,

Yet every man is flawed in some respect,

And all of us humans will sooner or later have a wreck

As that is the nature of man,

But we must forgive and unite, holding on with a friendly hand,

So wends the way of souls in tune with God,

Billowing on this Earth without deception or fraud;

Furthermore, we as Americans have finally proved

That from times uncouth we have trumped and beyond moved.

TWO:

Bill Clinton had an Achilles' heel,

But we hope that he did to God kneel,

Asking for forgiveness and growing a better name,

And maybe he has, having supported his wife in the political game,

But he was hope in a white man,

Sculpting with his politics a better plan

That all might unite and be one people

Within and under what is America's steeple,

And to think since his turbulent presidency

Of his vision now do us in this country see,

For we have finally trusted a black face,

Allowing it invitation into our living rooms with star-power grace.

Alas, I cannot blabber enough

About how determined and uncannily tough

Is the political machine of Barack Obama,

And may he bring justice to the haters like Osama;

Specifically, what now will those Theocratic states of Islam do?

For as Mahomet rose to heaven he said it's true

That all Africans are honorary Caliphs in a sense;

Hence, President Obama will have the reach, and it shouldn't be tense

Since under our red, white, and blue

Stands a Christian soldier that respects Islam through and through,

Loving the diversity of our planet Earth,

Not wanting sanguine circumstance to steal away our mirth,

For this world needs a leader

Who acts magnanimous and makes things clearer,

Having courage like Ronald Reagan's heart

To sit across from adversaries and pick them apart—

Just as Reagan fought the entire Cold War across a table

So will President Obama's victory be like a virgin birth in a luminous stable;

Specifically, Reagan fought an entire war without gore on the ground,

And President Obama too will be a wise pitcher on the mound,

Throwing not curveballs but rocketing the hot heat

That will intimidate and our enemies defeat,

Making them understand that if in these here States

We can gel our differences and embrace others' fates;

Then, maybe they too can cool on down,

Extinguishing their desire to spawn nuclear weapons with a frown

Upon their neighbors aglow with different skin and different laws;

Thus, already as a rookie will Barack Obama have a cause,

Which is to cool the heat of world leaders in love with themselves;

Alas, may Obama intently get them to put their nukes on the shelves.

THREE:

Gas prices arc through the roof;

Hence, maybe it's George W. Bush's brain gone uncouth,

For what's the big secret here?

Indeed, start a war with the Arabs and higher gas prices are clear,

And we all know that nobody in Iraq did the World Trade Center explode—

Verily, Bush ignited a war based on his theological code,

Believing that Jesus Christ would come to Earth,

Blasting the Arabs with spiritual missiles of girth;

Alas, Jesus remained in heaven

While Bush has his pick-up-truck revving,

And maybe Jesus talks to Mahomet in paradise—

These two religious leaders may over dinner both be nice,

For Mahomet was a prophet of the desert floor,

And with the assistance of the Arch-Angel Gabriel did he the Koran score

As a best seller, as is the Bible,

Both informing us that unto God we are liable;

Indeed, Mahomet knew Gabriel very well,

And Jesus' mother also thinks that Arch-Angel is swell;

Hence, the truth is clear to me

That Jesus and Mahomet would share a pee

At the urinal and start a manly chat,

Both hating the devil and many a leprous rat—

Truly, Christianity and Islam did appear

By way of the Jews being resilient and refusing to disappear

But staying strong based on their love for God,

And that exact same God does Jesus and Mahomet both bow and nod,

For Jesus claims that salvation comes from the Jews,

And Mahomet's prophecy is rooted in Ishmael's blues;

Therefore, all three of the major religions

Should embrace each other with sublime decisions,

And imagine how happy God would be

If these three faiths chopped down Eve's evil tree

And forged a union of faith and love;

Plus, imagine a Space Program that would take us above

The stratosphere and into space,

Where again would mankind start a pioneering race

To unite each other with a Federation made,

And make sure the Whore of Babylon is by our Union spayed,

For to bring peace to the Middle East

Must we construct and many spacecrafts be leased,

Revoking Palestinian's right to be aboard

If they continue with Israel to be attached with a hateful cord,

But cut the woes and these three religions go

Into space like a Star Trek show—

If this world would unite for space

So that we could explore and mine in many a place,

Jobs would be created, and we'd have a global goal

That would save all of us from paying a sanguine toll,

For if countries continued to attack and wage war;

Then, boot them out of the Federation's core;

Thus, they'd be humble and apologize

So again that their culture would the galaxy surmise

As back in ancient times when man was a pioneer;

Hence, we have to advance into space with no human fear.

FOUR:

Michelle Obama has taken many a hit,

Yet she is tough and doesn't fold and have a fit;

Plus, she's finally proud of her country,

Having witnessed America from being black like tea,

Full of health benefits and finally known

That ebony and ivory are both a yummy ice cream cone;

Indeed, she maybe said "Whitey" or not,

Yet all of us inwards may have a racial spot,

But it's about evolving beyond such a thing,

So that we can gel together and wear supermundane bling.

Verily, nothing is more scary than being afraid of another's pigment;

However, we must mix to exile racism, making it gone and sent

Into the Multiverse, where it will disperse,

No longer to our humanity being a curse;

Moreover, blacks are not better athletes than whites,

And whites are not smarter than blacks' intellectual mights,

For most black people can't play football like Steve Young,

And most white people can't talk smartly like Barack Obama's tongue;

Thus, we are more equal than does television display,

And to no one should this fact bring dismay,

But just like in the U.S. Army the only color is green,

So must we merge into one pulsating machine

That pumps the heart of our Country great,

Where Barack Obama has transcended the hate,

And now those from Africa can know for sure

That the time has come for racism's cure,

Yet there will always be haters hanging onto the fringe,

Swinging back and forth on a weak-minded hinge,

Not being concrete is outpacing bad taste,

Knowing that Barack Obama is more, being a black man laced

With a white mother, being true synergy,

Shining with both aspects of our majority;

Indeed, our country is ready to reveal

To the world that we have both types of appeal,

And even Hillary Clinton with her female form

Goes to show that in America, diversity is worn

By the red, white, and blue that Old Glory does brag,

And though there's still hatred with words like "Fag",

At least we are breaking down the stone

To a true Country of liberty that we wish to hone,

And indeed the Spirit of 1776 is alive,

Inspiring our different cultures to melt and thrive,

Billowing beyond the hate in the Middle East,

Proving that America deserves from God a blessed feast,

For we have listened to Dr. King and people like Kennedy,

Mixing our deaths so that we can be more free,

And to the whole world now may America prove,

That different colors mixed have the best groove;

Still, haters like Hitler will always exist in time,

By their own strength trying to destroy my rhyme,

Wanting everything to go the way of their fears

That they paint upon their victims with many sad tears;

Hence, like Jesus dieing for all

Must we force ourselves to always stand tall,

Spilling even our own damn blood

So that evil again won't ruin our world with a flood.

FIVE:

Britney Spears was fine a while ago,

Making every guy want a little some of her sexy ego;

Specifically, Britney was the finest piece of sass,

Having the galaxy's best ass,

And is more like Marilyn Monroe than you are;

Indeed, she was once a blonde, platinum star;

Moreover, with a myriad of conscious minds focusing their sex

Energy upon her does grant the young star a hex,

For goes the axiom that if millions of people are focusing on you

In like a carnal way—this launches a zoo

In the mind of the one being blown into a plethora of nervous pieces,

Taken apart like Humpty Dumpty and not the resilience of Jesus.

Verily, Britney has morphed macabre and haunts us eerie,

Yet of her beauty we won't grow weary,

Finding maybe satisfaction that she is not far from the trailer,

But hey, not just officers are good people, but too many a sailor

Adorned only in a Cracker Jack uniform,

Like Britney in the early millennia before her disfavoring storm.

And would androids develop conscious thought?

Making waves with fellow robotic siblings and the art anthropology fought

By way of these emotions making us combative,

Lasting as long as our pride does live,

Which is rebellion against God,

And now to snack on a piece of broiled cod

Before I pull the curtains and Britney does disappear,

Giving you the third-dimension to this book see more clear—

Like this,

Giving kismet a kiss:

Rolled back snug tight in the hills and a valley, resides pampered suburbia green in the Mid-South, and mysticism is happening there, being not sloppy magic, yet fine-crafted words made perverse by way of a spooky story to tell, spinning not a nasty yarn, but a tragic tale of eloquence lost, all for the sake of people without honor—

Did we enjoy the fall of Britney Spears,

Applauding her tears with our cheers?

Indeed, it seems we are envious of her,

Us not being able to look so hot and be adorned in the finest of fur;

Thus, we congratulate ourselves when someone pretty falls,

Not caring that through the loops of high school halls

Do we make our subject walk the plank to the principal's office,

Us being not an expert but a hellish novice,

Wanting to taste the defeat of total popularity;

Then, we can relax when the gold we do pee,

Passing gas as the urine is discharged,

Wanting our glory to be extra large,

And she falls like an angel with clipped wings,

Us insulting her and the way she sings,

Saying it was only for her face and body

That popularity did come knocking and myriads of boys made naughty;

Hence, the crime is upon our hands,

From where we did jerk, like primates on contraband—

Try having ten million people concentrate at the same time sexing you,

This will make you more than a shrew,

So spiritual world get a clue—

Sorcery and magic be real here like invisible dew

On the green lawns of the suburbs so plush,

And Britney's teenage body did reduce us to mush.

SIX:

Barack Obama won't love your mama

As would maybe Bill Clinton in his silky pajama;

Moreover, concerning Britney Spears and what her face is worth—

It could bring communication to the good, green Earth;

Indeed, Britney needs to be the Press Secretary for the Untied States,

For our Nation would be glued to television hearing our fates

From the bombshell and her lips so full,

Making men finally pay attention to what swims in the political pool,

And there are many sharks in such dangerous water;

Plus, there are charlatans who only project fodder—

Yes, Barack as President and Britney as Press Secretary—

This should not be insane; should not be scary,

For Barack's youth has plenty of truth,

And Britney is like Superman in the phone booth;

Alas, maybe I'm being a bit silly;

Still, look at how ludicrous was the White House with Slick Willy,

And I'm sorry Mr. Clinton for putting you down,

But you had your chance for greatness, and you let us down;

Specifically, you said Mary Jane should be legal;

However, myriads are in jail getting raped, and does cry the Eagle

Of America, where prohibition slaps Old Glory in the face,

Like spraying the red, white, and blue with a can of rank mace;

Furthermore, non-violent drug offenders getting raped in prison

Is like cutting the heart out of total liberty with precise incision;

Hence, maybe Barack will again freedom grant,

Taxing legal drugs so that we have more money and to rant

About where it will go, and what it will do;

Specifically, if to tax legal drugs our economic problems would be through;

Indeed, the United States could be rich again,

If the Christian Fundamentalists didn't view liberty as a sin,

For God gave us free will,

So what's the big deal if we swallow a pill?

And these Evangelicals really don't even like Jesus Christ,

Making His Mom lurid and spiced

By believing that a man's seed was deposited into her womb,

Not believing that she was God's lover and only to Him did zoom

With want, and fervent desire,

Knowing that only God could make her higher,

But Evangelicals praise Jesus and say He's the best,

Yet they slap the face of His mama and put shells into her Kevlar vest

Crafted by God as He protects Mary His love,

For at the tender age of fourteen did He touch her ovaries with a dove

So pure and inviolate, as He so much is;

Thus, how would He allow her to be sexed, when she is His bliss?—

So who is more wrong when it comes to Mary?

Indeed, she transcends humanity, like a fairy,

And God is in our image too;

Hence, after He made love to Mary how could He allow another to?

For God is great and a loyal mate,

And Mary is the one who He did date,

And Jesus Christ as today's science can prove

Was a 50% genetic twin to Mary's many a pure move—

Verily, Jesus is a blueprint of Mary,

And the other half of Him is from God, kinda scary,

But a demigod, being a biological son,

Shedding Mary's blood too, on the cross where it did run

Downwards and onto the Earth

As Mary witnessed without a spark of mirth,

Watching her child from the seed of God

Lower His head and to death did nod

While her eyes were burning with tears,

Losing an only son Who she raised for years—

Even Jesus Himself would say:

"You can talk about me, but don't you dare believe my Mom did lay

Any man, but only the great God in paradise."—

Truly, Mary is pure, clean of man, and ever so nice.

SEVEN:

Again, to peace in the Middle East will I ode,

Knowing that we need to make a prince from a toad—

It is true that Jew, Christian, and Muslim people

All worship the same God from under many a different steeple,

For the God of Israel is Who these three religions to submit;

Hence, why with each other do we have a big fit?

Specifically, the Jews believe that David is the Messiah,

And Christians believe it's Jesus, Who in His time was a pariah,

And the Muslims too believe in a Mahdi,

Each religion hoping that their Saints return with a key,

And while Christ zoomed upwards into heaven,

So did Mahomet like lucky number seven,

Yet King David died and was buried in the ground,

And with the science of today, we can resurrect him from the mound;

Furthermore, we can clone every body buried in the soil,

Resurrecting an exact genetic match that might crime try to foil,

For if the body of King David was cloned today,

In years to come would he be the identical man of yesterday?

And will the Democratic party in the future,

Pass laws to bring back the dead without needing a Frankenstein suture?

Truly, all people in graveyards could be cloned,

Proving the dogma of physical resurrection to be real and prone

To show our strength through science and might;

Hence, let's bring the dead back with a fight,

For legislation that would resurrect the dead,

Would be the greatest thought in mankind's head.

* * * * * *

Barack Obama is a merge

Of Martin Luther King being on the verge

Of genius, for Barack is both a white and black man,

Being the synergy of a dream—tall, dark, and tan;

Moreover, Britney Spears has problems indeed,

Yet we have lusted over her with greed

When she had yellow hair and danced in white,

Illuminating our fantasies with her effulgent bright,

And every man in America did fold

To a dream of Britney when the night got cold;

Specifically, even Bob Dole flirted with Britney on a t.v. add,

Her being the hottest, most shimmering fad—

So, as I bring Barack and Britney together,

Maybe my grandma is knitting a sweater,

For America is diverse with these two giants soaring like a kite,

And never should succeeding give us fright,

For forward into the America day,

Must we march like soldiers, and like unto pure priests pray.

EIGHT:

The planet Mars needs to be explored,

For we might mine its geography, getting its resources scored,

And imagine the jobs that this would produce,

Forging millions of workers never to be loose,

Building spacecraft galore and crew members many,

Taking from the Red Planet a very pretty penny,

But we refuse to embrace the space above,

Treating the Earth with all our anchored love,

Forsaking our own evolution,

Stuck in the mire of our own confusion;

Indeed, there is more than the Earth;

Thus, to mine our planetary neighbors might bring worth.

Anyway, how much longer must I give ode,

Spilling the beans and burping like a toad,

But we are pioneers and shouldn't forget

That it would be glorious to upon Mars' shore wreck

A ship, and shut the motor down,

Putting the smile on an innocent clown—

One that doesn't kill with a sinister glare

But thieves away a child's despair;

Moreover, don't even get me started on clowns,

For my phobia of the circus is like being hunted by hounds

Hungry for my flesh and all the rest;

Hence, explore the Multiverse with human zest

And let us be the gods that King David spoke about,

Morphing into superhumans without a doubt,

For in the future, if we live,

Humanity will become immortal and give

Ourselves a pat on the back

Before cloning the souls lost to the rack

And all the rest, resurrecting with our science the dead body of man

So that of God we can become a bigger fan;

Furthermore, be not a fool,

For God has technology that would make man drool,

It even having organic mechanics,

Being cooler than a private eye t.v. show like Mannix,

But Simon and Simon and Magnum P.I.

Were the best shows, yet Jim Rockford didn't lie,

And I want to drive a Firebird with a V-8 as well;

Therefore, we must mine Mars if in its fuel tank will energy dwell—

So goes I, barding my pestering song,

And even something tiny can blaze like something long,

For less is more in many a case,

And if you don't believe me; then on your food lace

With a bit of butter and cream

Not clogging your arteries as much and giving your face a puffy mien;

Indeed, even a fool can birth brilliance aglow,

Just like many a late night comedian on a talk show—

Now, wend with me to better understand the ghost of man,

And my man Obama, you'd better get a space plan.

NINE:

America's economy can be fixed

If with the Holy Spirit of 1776 does our country again get with mixed;

Specifically, legalizing drugs and taxing the smoke

Would provide a fortune of money for our country gone broke;

Indeed, the economy would boom and we'd be more free;

Plus, much of the depressed would have access to glee,

But drugs do freak and scare many people,

Especially those who believe God's heart feeble,

Yet this is liberty at its best,

Making Old Glory blow in the wind and rest,

Knowing freedom oozes red, white, and blue,

Bleeding the joy of a theocracy being ended and through,

For our Country should not be run by morals and laws,

But cascading forth freedom that does liberty cause;

However, we're afraid of such a leap,

Preferring a bad economy to further seep

Down in the gutter as we are broke,

The bigger evil being our borrowing so much from others as if a joke,

For we should be able to stand on our own two feet,

Teaching the world how to theocracy defeat,

Like in many a Muslim country where alcohol will get you killed

If you secretly get buzzed from a six pack and totally thrilled—

How stupid these theocracies that prohibit booze,

Meaning if we don't legalize and tax; then we'll also loss,

Being a mirror image of a Muslim country ruled by God's angry fist;

Thus, better for liberty to be breathed and by God's mercy kissed.

* * * * * *

THE CONVERSATION FOR OUR FREEDOM:

MISTER LIBERTY

Hey, like why so truculent?

MR. THEOCRACY

Our country must be ruled with God in mind. Drugs are evil, and total liberty is anarchy.

MISTER LIBERTY

Like King David said: "Wine to make man's heart happy, and herb for the service of man." Too, God gave us free will—so who the hell is the government to take it away with strict laws?

MR. THEOCRACY

God must be the Nation of Man!

MISTER LIBERTY

Take a chill pill.

MR. THEOCRACY

A pill?—Never . . .

MISTER LIBERTY

Look, the government of the United States has no right to declare war upon its own people. And that's what the Drug War is—a declaration of war from the American government upon its own people.

MR. THEOCRACY

God trumps government; thus, He should be the leader of the United States.

MISTER LIBERTY

Yeah, but look at how Bush played it. He thought Jesus would come back and help him fight the Arabs. Lincoln prayed constantly as President, but he shot down prohibition as well as the involvement of trans-corporeal life in politics—as far as he could glimpse anyway.

MR. THEOCRACY

You will burn in hell.

MISTER LIBERTY

Just like Mark David King wrote in his poetic book entitled: "Sean Hannity's theocracy; plus, Virgin Mary LIVES"—If God gets in the way of freedom; then He is not perfect, but liberty is.

MR. THEOCRACY

Oh Mama Mia—you're going to burn in hell.

MISTER THEOCRACY

I already went there, but they kicked me out for selling ice cream.

Part Two: The Cyborg Is Created—

ONE:

Just a dandy teenage boy, and he likes the girls,

Loving their fleshy skin; plus, it's even better if their hair has curls;

Anyway, disaster does strike every man

As goes our humanity cursed by the adder's plan,

And that boy named Rikki

Fell in the shower and got damaged super trickie,

Needing his loins amputated by a doctor with a smirk,

Rikki knowing that this surgeon was a jerk,

Cracking a joke to the nurses before he removed the teenage p%*#@,

Pissing off every god, including the beauty of Venus;

Still, every doctor has something decent inside,

And the physician would reconstruct Rikki's libido-like hide,

Forging onto his form without a rod,

A ten-thousand dollar member that health care didn't agree to with a nod,

And Rikki's father intent upon his son's bliss

Did take out a second mortgage so that his son might one day kiss;

Furthermore, a robotic attachment that was a vibrating piece

Was screwed into Rikki, like on a golf course with a pond some geese;

Hence, now he could love a girl;

However, he wouldn't feel anything after his pants would unfurl,

And as he came home from the hospital room,

He knew his appendage was like a witch's broom;

Moreover, Rikki's Dad was still upset,

For the health care plan's denial wouldn't let

That family rest without economic trouble,

Them having to sacrifice so that their son wouldn't be estranged in a bubble.

Verily, Rikki needed that sophisticated attachment, it's true,

But his health care plan not paying made him and his family blue,

For like a eunuch would he have been without the robot member,

And the insurance company that didn't pay was run by a greedy spender;

Specifically, the insurance said it was not a necessity,

Yet a cosmetic surgery that had to do with vanity.

Now, how in the world could insurance deny

A boy without a complete package that cries to God, "Why?"???

Indeed, Rikki's Dad had always been a Republican through and through,

But after the insurance denied Rikki's surgery, with that party he truly knew,

Knowing every Democrat would want a teenager to be covered with care

If their love muscle was traumatized with overwhelming despair;

Moreover, many a Republican would just grin and say "Bear it",

Them thinking lovemaking is only for many a rabbit;

Still, this is not to say every Republican is evil,

For many of them bow to God like Saints in times medieval.

It's just that health insurance companies don't give a rat's ass

About the suffering of so many with stuff like psychiatric gas;

Specifically, if you have mental illness or need cosmetic surgery,

Insurance companies will fly away from you like a selfish birdie,

For one bad thing about Capitalism

Is the fact that many a wealthy person will start a Schism

If even a bit of their money is taken away;

Therefore, to a Good God must we pray,

Knowing that money is not the most important thing;

Alas, tear down the philosophy of those in love with bling.

TWO:

After his robotic part had finally healed and been permanently fused,

Rikki went back to high school, him hearing jokes and getting accused

Of having Darth Vader in his blue jeans;

Still, some girls were nice, fantasizing erotic scenes

With the cyborg boy and his expensive loins

That made many wish for him, like throwing in a fountain coins;

Moreover, the guys all made fun and teased the boy,

Them kind of jealous of his machine-like toy

That was a glowing, liquid metal design,

Growing in length like a rapper does rhyme,

But Rikki endured the jeers with steel,

Knowing that toughness has great appeal;

Still, he was hurt and a little sad,

But a shrink gave him anti-depressants that made him glad.

Still, the insurance companies wouldn't even cover his shrink's bill,

For they didn't think psychiatry was worthy like the pill

That Rikki took everyday,

And this again made his Dad's heart sway,

Hating the mammon of rich guys in fancy suits,

Wanting to pull their hair out by the roots,

And even baldness doesn't get covered by health care,

Which can make a man of his self-consciousness be aware;

Indeed, life sometimes is a thick, poop sandwich,

And we have to eat the e-coli like a runny Manwich,

But Sloppy Joes to some are good and hearty,

Even though they may make you farty,

And Rikki's Dad did develop a gastrointestinal disease,

Him so nervous from begging the insurance companies with pleas of please;

Still, he had to pay for everything himself,

Wondering if the Bible on his living room shelf

Had an answer to all this trauma

That had affected his life with sincere, crappy drama,

Forcing the man to get a second job,

Where he scooped ice cream with a humble nod,

Sweating bullets from labor, all for his son

Since the insurance companies wouldn't make life fun,

And while Rikki had endured more than his share,

It was his father that suffered in his lair,

Locking himself in his bedroom at night,

And on his knees to God about his money-crunching plight,

Begging the Lord to let him not lose his house

All because his son lost his genitalia and made Daddy a souse,

For Rikki's father began to drink,

And he too went to see a shrink;

Moreover, health insurance again didn't pay,

Giving the hard-working man a wrinkle of dismay.

Verily, what the blast is going on,

And why am I barding such a twisted song?

It's axiomatic that if you lose a dong;

Then, insurance should pay no matter how small or long,

For genital mutilation can be worse than death,

And you'll never be happy like a crack whore on meth;

Furthermore, Rikki's Dad was tired and abused

From working two jobs without being amused,

But giving all his wages to that second mortgage pay;

Next, drinking in his room, and on his knees to pray,

Finding God after a bottle of wine

Just like King David said so fine:

"Wine to make man's heart happy; herb for the service of man.!!!"

Truly the mystical text of psalms offered a better health plan

Than those conservatives like sticks in mud,

Not giving a pink twinkie about others' crud,

For as long as they can make and hoard their money;

Then life is fine, and they think this funny,

Yet as Jesus instructed a man to be poor,

This kind of story makes Republicans sore,

And damn, I'm not saying that Democrats have more class,

Yet when it comes to human suffering they are like a Catholic Mass,

Knowing that mercy is sincerely majestic indeed,

And Rikki's new package made him like a normally-constructed steed,

Yet at night when his hormones would command,

And that teenage boy had to wrap a hand

Around that appendage made of science bizarre,

He felt sick in his stomach, seeing himself as a falling star

Lost to being a cyborg that may freak a lady;

Hence, he didn't have the nerve to make a pass at a chick named Katie,

For she was all flesh, and he saw himself as a machine,

Having the penile countenance of Darth Vader's polished gleam;

Thus, Rikki did dream very far away

Into the future, where his heart did pray,

Hoping technology would catch up fast

So that in love he may endure and last,

Being engaged maybe to an android girl

Who would love him with kisses and on hot legs twirl,

Dancing with him into paradise;

Indeed, Rikki's dreams were so fluidic and nice.

THREE:

THE SHRINK

So Rikki, how are you feeling?

RIKKI

Like a suffering extra in the Brothers Karamazov.

THE SHRINK

Oh, you find joy and peace in mystical, Russian literature?

RIKKI

I like the character Kalganov, and how he talks about how it is better to live

in an imaginary world over the real world.

THE SHRINK

Have you been doing that?

RIKKI

I have no choice, for what girl would ever love a cyborg like me?

THE SHRINK

There are other things in life besides romance.

RIKKI

I just want a girlfriend so bad, but I know that I'm a freak.

THE SHRINK

Everybody is a freak on some level. Look kiddo, you must force yourself to
be positive. That's all you can do. No matter how far into the dumps you
get, just force yourself to be positive; being positive built the world, and
negativity is always attempting to tear it down.

RIKKI

Some things need to be torn down, like a stupid kid with a robotic private
part.

THE SHRINK

I don't want to hear that from you Rikki; you are a nice boy, and I'm sure if
you desire a mate that it will happen for you. Be patient and trust in a
merciful God.

RIKKI

Why did God let this happen? How could he allow me to get mutilated?

THE SHRINK

You know, plenty of girls may like that technology which you possess
behind your trousers. There used to be a show on television called "The Six
Million Dollar Man", it telling the tale of an amputee who gets bionic
appendages; indeed, like him, maybe your libido machine is superior to a
real, fleshy organ.

RIKKI

I just hate myself sometimes doctor.

THE SHRINK

Like I said kiddo, you need to force yourself to be positive. Do it!

FOUR:

I (author of poetasterism) have been harassed by many a collection agency,

For I had run up bills due to being crazy;

Specifically, my Ulcerative Colitis was bleeding me dry,

And my Obsessive Compulsive Disorder did merge with Psychosis and fly

Me to the hospital many times,

Where I had blood transfusions, chemo-like infusions, and penned rhymes;

Still, of being sick and not able to pay

Collection agencies pestered me night and day,

And I was barely a hundred pound man;

Plus, I even had a decent health care plan;

Nevertheless, all my medicines, the myriads I took,

In the end did make me forsook,

For when OCD does haunt the brain,

Dealing with threats did drive me insane,

And I broke a beer bottle over my face,

Sending me to the emergency as if in a race

To stop the bleeding and stitch me together;

Nonetheless, the collections agencies continued on like stormy weather;

Moreover, what about the tons of folk who suffer worse than me,

Like a man with a kidney stone who can't go pee,

And then when he does, it's like giving birth;

Thus, only by way of a morphine drip does he get mirth.

Sorry for steering away from Rikki,

Who felt so bad that he might never get a hickie,

For how to expose a robotic part to a girl

Without making her run to the sink and hurl?

But he exists, somewhere in time,

Like a tear on a clown or sad-hearted mime;

Alas, Obama take the lead,

And make it so that you stop the bleed

Of blues and melancholy due to affording your health,

Which all could be covered if drugs were legal and on a shelf;

Specifically, make drugs legal and tax their cost;

Next, everyone would be covered and never lost,

Yet true liberty is too much for Republicans

Since they think drugs are related to sins,

Not remembering the Holy Spirit of 1776

When all was legal, and Washington got blitzed;

Furthermore, did Lincoln put down prohibition,

Saying that it was like theocracy fish'n;

Indeed, we need money for our economy;

Also, we must remember that we are a country free

As did Roosevelt who gave us liquor

After the graphic violence of Eliot Ness was quicker

Than even a cowboy's swift pistol pull,

Yes, prohibition causes gangs and fools

To get killed, and cops do too,

But if our country was free, gangs would be through,

Making drug dealers have to get real jobs,

Where they might make an honest living and be snobs

As goes the beloved irony of it all;

Thus we must be like Lincoln, and hear freedom's call.

FIVE:

John McCain must be mentioned too,

For that dude was a bad ass, it's true;

Plus, his wife is gorgeous indeed,

And his Vice Presidential Running Mate can motor like a steed;

However, their problem is the war in Iraq

That drains our economy and puts pressure on our back—

We've already won, and leaving is not retreat,

For that would only be if only Saddam we didn't defeat,

Yet Osama is the real nasty sucker

Who would rape our American Women with a terror-like pucker;

Hence, if we spend money to hunt;

Next, knock the real enemies out of the park and don't bunt

A ball that barely rolls,

Our involvement in Iraq costs like unjust tolls;

Still, maybe McCain is correct about drilling,

For our country in size trumps Arab Nations by millions;

Indeed, Alaska is larger than most of Arabia,

And there are many college girls here with a pierced labia—

So Obama you should think about our black gold,

Which did allow the Beverly Hillbillies to California be sold.

* * * * * *

A CONVERSATION WITH THE INCARNATION OF THE HOLY GHOST—

Dramatis Personae

MANI: Persia's greatest painter, having been visited by his angelic twin during adolescence; moreover, is the Living Holy Ghost that Jesus the Christ said would descend upon the Earth. Mani taught the truth of asceticism, including vegetarianism, sexual repression, and severe intellectual knowledge in order to break through to the Empyreal Place where the Good God does reside; unfortunately, because of his teachings, Mani was beheaded and his body stuffed with straw where it was then hung on a city wall so that all might resist his true sublimity.

MARTIN LUTHER: Like Siddhartha who inherited a coinhabitant known as the Cosmic Buddha, this one time Catholic resisted asceticism and the pious lifestyle, founding Protestantism and a true contempt for the inviolate Womb of the Blessed Virgin Mary that did spawn the Christ.

HERE WE GO—

MARTIN LUTHER

Selling Indulgences—ashamed should the Catholic Church be for such

lunacy, stuffing their pockets with the hard–earned money of others.

MANI

Look, if you get sick—you see a physician; if you get in legal trouble—you

see an attorney; thus, if you need God, you see a priest; hence, paying a

Church full of ascetics and mystics who do nothing all day long but attempt

to communicate with the Holy God in order to usher in a prayer for your

money is a magnanimous thing.

MARTIN LUTHER

Hogwash. And, we are saved by faith alone, as I have proved from the

Scriptures.

MANI

Yes, but it was the Catholics who put those Holy Scriptures in order as they

are, having four Gospels just as there are four winds so did wend the

vociferousness of Saint Irenaeus; furthermore, why elevate the Letters of

Paul over the Gospels of the Messiah, Christ? God is not limited to the

Bible; God transcends even the Bible, and the first few centuries after Christ

there was many a Holy Text architected by ascetic, Catholic men, those same men and their spiritual seeds keeping the Holy Church alive for

centuries despite the Great Schism and the Reformation you launched all

because you could not handle living an ascetic lifestyle. You gave up Mr.

Luther. Too, you stole from the purity of Mary, and now, we have a myriad

of folk who believe that the pure womb of Mary did receive the injection of

a manly seed; on the contrary, after God touched her virginal ovaries at the

tender age of fourteen, she was His, and her womb forever protected by the

holy angels. Truly, Protestantism slaps the mother of Jesus on her

immaculate countenance; plus, it robs the followers of the God of Israel of

being able to invoke those not dead, but alive in Christ to pray for us here

who live on Earth. Also, it rejects the ability to invoke the angelic lifeforms

ranked within the Celestial Hierarchy—now, how is asking Saint Michael

the Arch-Angel, or Saint Mary the mother of God to pray for you an evil

thing? For does not God hear two voices better than one. Catholicism is the

last ascetic lifestyle, where people like Saint Francis of Assisi threw himself

in the thorn bushes for having a sexual thought, and Saint Jerome learned the

Hebrew language in order to steal away his masculine mind from visions of

bare-naked ladies—these kinds of men are not saved by faith alone, yet they

will cut off any part of their flesh that makes them sin, as commanded Jesus,

unlike the Protestants who shy away from asceticism in order to have a more peaceful life. And what of a legion of Nuns who cut off their noses so that the barbarians who invaded their village would not find them attractive and rape them?—They did that holy action in order to preserve their immaculate wombs, which trumps the zero action of many a Protestant thinking that just his belief in Jesus gets them to Heaven—what insanity. For does not even the devil himself believe that Jesus is the Christ; thus, will the devil make it to Heaven? Nope, not unless by his actions he begins to embrace and bless humanity; indeed, I have just proved that "By Faith Alone" is a fantasy for the weak, just as you were when you pooped on the Church of God in order to have an easier lifestyle.

MARTIN LUTHER

Who are you to say this, and why? For didn't the Catholics shut up you and that quasi-Gnosticism?

MANI

Yep, but I still know what is right. Exorcism too, by way of invoking Saint Michael and Jesus Christ, another ritual thought foolish by you.

MARTIN LUTHER

Why are you doing this?

MANI

To undo what you have done. Look, I know that you had intestinal problems and even passed gas in front of the Pope, but like suck it up and engage asceticism. Be a trooper for Christ instead of simply just believing in Him, for while He may be the Truth, the Path, the Life—that means kicking your own ass to stay straight and not be swayed. Damn't Martin Luther, suffer for the sake of Christ.

SIX:

Sarah Palin is a fox

Even though her jaw is shaped like a box;

Indeed, she will be a political force in America's future,

Making other dames like Hillary have to more beauty suture

Upon themselves in order to compete,

For having good looks is a talent and treat

Just as it is with being tall and strong

Or having the pipes to shout out an awesome song—

We all have gifts and must use them right

In order for our world to evolve and unite.

Too, there's nothing wrong with Protestantism's light,

But don't put down other people because you think you're right;

Moreover, we are all right,

If we serve a Holy Purpose and act like Superman in flight.

God doesn't care if you're a Jew, Christian, Muslim, whatever—

Just suffer for the sake of your conscience and don't be a quitter.

* * * * * *

So, Barack Obama wants health care

And Sarah Palin wants to drill with no despair;

Also, Obama might not get pissed at gay pride

While Palin may say that's a skanky side

And she may be right, but we have to pick and choose,

Knowing that liberty should live here and cruise

Within the theater of great minds whether black or white,

For all of us suffer a monstrous plight—

Some of us may have good looks, while others have money,

And some might be philosophical as others are funny;

Specifically, we should just love our country and preserve the free

Spirit of all, even greenie weenies trying to save a tree—

Just don't have sex like a nympho and others' morals overthrow,

For we must control ourselves like the grass in a yard we mow,

And speaking of grass, why the hell does that get you raped up the ass?

Truly, we are free and should be, but wise enough not to sass,

And while African-Americans are just as good,

Many a brother in the county jail is a hood

And wants to make your time worse

By painting your ass with lipstick and making you carry a purse.

Why can't the criminal do his time in peace

Instead of getting his pants in an unnatural crease?

What I'm saying—DON'T BE AN ANIMAL,

Yet respect your freedom and eat it like a cannibal,

Resisting broken marriages, short skirts, and Internet porn,

For while we are free this does give God some scorn

And rightfully so,

For the hedonist spawns an unnatural woe.

SEVEN:

Black or white—it doesn't matter. Just don't be an ass. Man or woman—

doesn't matter. Just don't abuse your physical virtue. Druggie or sober—

doesn't matter. And again, just don't be a jerk. Whatever you are, and whatever gifts you possess, use them to build the world, not tear it down. None is better than God, and we all must morph ourselves angelic, evolving to His level of thoughts and cognizance, for that is the true nature of man, to grow into a god himself, loving and caring for all those underneath his immediate power and prowess. Later dudes,

Mark David King

Epilogue:

Blessed are the confessors;

Moreover, here I go:

PRIEST

You're here because the Christ gave His Disciples the power to forgive sins, and I imitate the Celibate Hands of Him.

MARK

Bless me Father, for I have sinned—it has been two decades since my last confession.

PRIEST

Judas Priest!

MARK

I looked at a dirty website a few times; plus, I did tricked a blue parrot into saying some profane utterances, and there was a watermelon incident; at the same time, I've practiced celibacy and asceticism—locked myself in closets, gave myself minor concussions, and many facial stitches. But damn, I just feel so unholy; I've talked on the Internet and phone to a few shady characters, and I wrote erotic poetry to many folk, but I'd cut my Jesse Jackson's off before I would do anything fruity—oh Pandemonium, I'm freaking there, somebody strangle me. And yeah, I've broken some household furniture—did I mention the blue parrot yet?

PRIEST

Yeppers . . .

MARK

Still, I'm so physically pure that you could sacrifice me; nonetheless, I suck at life, and I don't have Free Will; if I did, I would freely resist sin at all times, yet the seed has to come out as a woman menstruates, and I'm, in a Levite Sense, unclean at times. But back to Free Will—if I had it, I would defy the Fallen Arch-Angelic contempt known as gravity, no more erotic thoughts and fluidic dreams; plus, no more red meat.

PRIEST

Do ten Hail Mary invocations—and mean it buster!!!

* * * * * *

I feel terrified at having crafted this somewhat odd piece of my own
personal, intellectual property, for I have been incarcerated for my poetry in
the past; however, there is no (1.) Fighting Words, (2.) Clear and Present
Danger; plus, it falls under something (3.) Ambiguous; hence, I have broken
no laws on this day. And, one more thing about the Virgin Mary—she had
to be perfect, for Jesus is a 50% genetic duplicate of her in every way, and at
least half of her had to ramble through this life on a level of perfection.
That's it, I guess. Oh yeah, may God grant you life and health—and that
goes for our new President as well. Shake the Pillars of Heaven Mr. Obama,
just like F.D. R. did, especially by giving us back our beer and wine, and
even Jesus brewed liquor—probably a nice Pinot Noir, you think . . .

- fini -

www.ingramcontent.com/pod-product-compliance
Lightning Source LLC
Chambersburg PA
CBHW022344040426
42449CB00006B/715